MY
MEMORIES
OF

To Terry

Best Wishes

From John Paul

Copyright © 2022 by John Paul Moore

Table of contents

Seeing Someone Someday 1

You And I 2

Time Together 3

When We Were Together 4

The Two of Us 5

Cold Christmas' 6

Snow Falling 7

My Favourite Time 8

When We 9

Day Dreading 10

I Wonder Now 11

Empty Streets 12

How Could I 13

I Wonder Was I 14

1995 15

Expressing Each Other's Love 16

Drinking Days 17

Your Time 18

Ruined Relationship 19

Did You Say 20

Thinking Time 21

Do I Want To 22

I Wonder Who 23

You Were 24

Christmas Day 25

Christmas Day Acrostic 26

New Year's Day Acrostic 27

I Saw You Standing 28

I Haven't Heard 29

Mr. Meredith 30

I Once Had You 31

Cards Can Be 32

Summer Acrostic 33

Winter Acrostic 34

I Was With you 35

Did you like me? 36

You Really Surprised Me? 37

Sometimes 38

I Saw You There? 39

I Have What You Don't Have? 40

There Was 41

I Sit Here 42

Was I Supposed To? 43

I Thought Being With You? 44

I've Seen You 45

Seeing Someone Someday

I am sitting here beside you,
I am going to a new country with you,
I thought that we were going to last long,
I thought that our relationship was so strong.

I really didn't get to know you as well as I wanted to,
A day I'll remember is when we went to Dublin Zoo,
I miss having someone to talk to like you,
Did I really have you?

I might one day find someone that I could call mine,
Did you think that breaking up with me was fine?
Why did you break up with me?
Did I get to know why you did leave me?

You And I

You and I, it wasn't the first time I had you,
You and I made us together for a long time,
You told me that your favourite drink didn't include a lime,
I had someone to express my feelings to once I was with you.

I don't know what made me to be with you,
I couldn't imagine my life without you,
I was so welcomed to stay at your place,
I was delighted that you also stayed at my place.

I miss these days where I would be holding you hand,
You and I got to see "Picture This" who was our favourite band,
I didn't like what you did to me,
If you didn't like me, then why where you with me.

I wonder who told you to leave me,
Did you not like being with me,
Of course, I could tell that you hated me,
What will your life be without me?

Time Together

My time with you was a blast,
Our time together went so fucking fast,
I enjoyed spending my time with you,
I don't know why I fucked up my time with you.

The time I had with you was the best I ever had,
It was until you left me for another fucking lad,
The day it happened I was left all alone,
Of course, when you did that to me, I did have a fucking moan.

Did I ever taught that I would be with you?
Of all the people in the world why did it have to be you,
I do miss having someone like you,
It was the best time of my life once I was with you.

What would I do to be with you,
Why would I change my life to be with you?
I don't know why you had to go and see another fucking lad,
I thought that you said that I was the best one you ever had.

When We Were Together

Why did you do it to me,
What made you do it to me,
I was delighted once I was with you,
I couldn't say that I didn't enjoy my time with you.

The time I had with you was the best I ever had,
Why would I change the clocks back to be with you?
I'm still complexed of why you left me for another lad,
This wasn't the first time I caused a fight with you.

You did say that you were with me to please me,
What would you do to get back with me,
I wasn't expecting to last that long with you,
I couldn't be more delightful that I'm not with you.

Do you want to know what happened to me when you broke up with me?,
I bet you don't want to know what happened to me,
I don't know why you were staring at me like that,
I will remember every time that we went on video chat.

I was mostly annoyed being with you,
It used to make me angry all the time when you rang me coming home from work,
Did I miss you when I wasn't being beside you?
I enjoyed our lovely phone calls to you when I was coming home from work.

The Two of Us

The two of us are lying in my bed,
I listened closely to every word that you had to say,
I listened closely to every word you said,
I thought that you said you wanted to stay.

I don't know why you did this to me,
I thought that you enjoyed being in my company with me,
I thought that the two of us were going to last long,
Don't ask me what I did wrong.

I thought that our relationship was so strong,
You said to me that "Perfect" by Ed Sheeran was your favourite song,
You said to me that something big could happen one day,
I was looking forward to finding out what was that day.

It puzzled me to know what that day could be,
I wonder will that day eventually happen to me,
I wonder will I ever find someone to be with me,
Do you think I will find someone to be with me?

I stroll around this place all on my own,
I don't know why you had to ring me on my phone,
I asked myself is this place better on my own,
We would regularly have a moan.

Cold Christmas'

My feet are bear standing on this cold floor,
I wonder why I'm standing here in the cold,
I don't know I was standing here out in the cold,
I don't know why I was standing bare foot on the floor.

I wonder will I get to see some snow falling outside,
I went out to make a snow angel, but I thought to myself well at least I tried to make one,
I wonder was there any snow falling near the seaside,
I don't know why I was wondering if there was any snow falling because there was none.

Was I dreaming about the snow coming down?
Was I dreaming about the snow coming down and covering up the whole town,
I hope that the snow will be on its way for one day,
I hope that it does snow for Christmas Day.

I would one day like to light up the whole house in these Christmas lights,
Maybe one day that Christmas Day will land on a Friday,
I saw someone in a shop picking up a box of Christmas lights,
I was hoping that there might be more snow found in Norway.

Snow Falling

I wonder will Jack Frost be out tonight,
I got a glimpse of some snow falling in the flickering of the light,
Seeing you falling puts a smile on my face,
I've always wanted snow falling around my place.

I love it when you are coming down,
I like seeing you covering up our whole town,
I don't want to see you falling down every single day,
The only time that I want to you falling is Christmas Day.

I wonder will there be snow falling today,
I wonder will the children be happy with snow falling today,
I wonder do you feel the cold,
I know that you don't feel the cold.

My Favourite Time

This season is one of my favourite times of the year,
I really enjoy seeing everyone's house lit up with so many Christmas lights,
That is why I love this time of the year,
I wonder will every house be displaying their Christmas lights.

I wonder can they see their houses from a far,
I glanced around and saw a shining star,
I wonder will people decorate their neighbour's car,
Was I dreaming about that shining star?

I really enjoy seeing snow,
I really enjoy seeing some patches of ice,
I don't know why people hate seeing snow,
Seeing you falling down covering up our village makes it look so nice.

When We

When you broke up with me,
I dragged myself into a hole,
I thought that you said that you loved me,
When I was with you, we used to go on a stroll.

When I was with you, we used to skip the odd class,
I don't know why we used to skip the odd class,
You were beside me for most of the time,
When we skipped the odd class, we would be missing for a long time.

I got to say that I loved you when I was with you,
I could say that I didn't really love you,
Every time I said that I loved you, you didn't say it back to me,
I was complexed why that you lasted that long with me.

The two of us lasted an extremely long time,
Why did you have to send me a text when you were beside me all the time,
I was surprized that you didn't even go halves on things with me all the time.

One of the days that I will remember is when we walked past the "London Eye,
When you broke up with me you didn't get to say goodbye,
I will always be grateful for the time I had with you,
Did I get to hear you say that you loved me.

Day Dreading

I was dreading this day to come,
I wonder why how this day did start,
I wasn't expecting this day to come,
I sit here having my favourite desert apple tart.

I wonder why what made this day to come,
Was it the fact that I wasn't suitable for you?
Was it my fault that this day will come?
I don't know why you were blaming me for it as it was you.

Why was I thinking of being blamed for doing it as it wasn't even me?
You must have seen this day coming as I didn't even know about it, you caught me texting someone else and asked me "Who is she?",
I don't want to remember the day that we did split.

I Wonder Now

I wonder now would I still be with you,
If I was still with you, what effect would it have it on me,
Do I regret being with you,
I still haven't found out why you left me.

I still haven't found out what made you break up with me,
I saw the odd smile from you when you were with me,
I knew something was wrong with you,
Was I enjoying my time with you?

I'm now all alone on Christmas Day,
I remember the day when I asked you out,
The day when I asked you out was the day after St. Stephen's Day,
I was happy when I asked you out.

Empty Streets

I wonder if these streets are better now on my own,
I used to wonder these streets with you,
I think that I could get used to these streets all on my own,
The two of us looked up and saw that the sky was blue.

These empty streets are better now the way they are,
I was enjoying these empty streets with you,
I think that I could get used to these empty streets the way they are,
Was I enjoying these empty streets with you?

I wonder why these streets are bear,
Why are these streets becoming bear?
I don't want these empty streets to be empty for long,
Did the two of us really go out for that long.

How Could I

How could I ever afford a house up in those hills,
Those houses must of cost too many bills,
I've always wanted to live up there,
The houses up there wouldn't be too far away from Maddison Square.

How am I going to afford going to Las Vegas?
I've been told that Las Vegas is a bad place,
I wonder I ever go to see this place,
Maybe one day I will get to go to Las Vegas.

How will I ever pay for a house up in those hills,
I bet those houses must of cost too many bills,
I don't know why I am here,
I wonder will I ever be here.

I Wonder Was I

I wonder was I supposed to be with you,
Why did I choose to be with you?
You must of saw something in me,
Were you happy being with me?

I told you that I wasn't with someone for that long,
Our time together lasted long,
Did I get to do things when I was you?
What was it that made me choose to be with you?

1995

I don't remember much about the year I was born,
I do know that it was the year I was born,
I've got photos to remind me of the year I was born,
Looking back at them photos that I have of myself it wasn't that long ago since I was born.

I haven't the foggiest of what happened that year,
I do know that I was born in July of that year,
I do know that it was the year that I came alive,
I was lucky to be born in the year 1995.

I like looking back at the things that happened the year I was born,
When I was younger, I was told that Blackburn Rovers won the league the year I was born,
I like looking back at photos of myself when I was young,
Looking back at my school photos I was so young.

Expressing Each Other's Love

I hope you expressed your love for me,
The same why I did for you,
I found out that you were only using me,
Of course, I didn't do that to you.

Why did you have to break my fucking heart?
I hope that you are better now,
I don't know why that you had to break my heart,
I wonder are the two of you happy now.

Did I get to see your house lit up with your Christmas lights,
I hope that he gets to see your house lit up in those Christmas lights,
I hope that he says that he loves you,
What made you not say it to me that I love you.

Did I know that we were going to last a fucking long time?
Did I want to be with you for a long time,
I think that you got to see the better side of me,
Why did you fucking use me?

Look at what you did to me,
I'm harmful for what you did to me,
I hope you think he's better than me,
What made you fucking leave me?

Do I want to know who told you to leave me?
Or do I want to know who told you to leave me,
If you didn't want to be with me,
Then why where you with me.

Drinking Days

I drank occasionally with you throughout our time,
I enjoyed drinking with you during our time,
Did I enjoy my time drinking with you?
I had a great time drinking with you.

I had a great time drinking with you,
I got to know more about you during our time,
It made me feel how much I really loved you,
I was only getting started to know you throughout our time.

Did you enjoy drinking with me,
You liked it when I would buy you a drink and you would say is that for me,
I was reminding you that I did love you and I was hoping that you would say it back to me,
Did I enjoy your drinking time with you?

Your Time

Was I really with you for a long time,
I don't know why our relationship lasted a long time,
Was I not the one for you?
Now I can officially blame you.

I couldn't care less if you are happy now,
Is there a reason why I'm even thinking about you now?
You could tell that I was playing around with it,
That is why the two of us did split.

Ruined Relationship

Our relationship lasted a long time,
Was I really with you for that amount of time,
I wasn't happy of what you did to me,
What was it that you didn't see in me?

Is that why you had to leave me,
Did you even care about what you did to me?
What made you leave me,
I wasn't crying when you fucking left me.

Did You Say

Did you say to me that you were the one?
I told you that you weren't the only one I had,
Why did you tell me that you were going to be the one?
You had to leave me for another lad.

Why did you leave me for another lad?
You told me that I wasn't the only one you ever had,
You told me that I might've been the one,
How come you told me that you were going to be the one.

Thinking Time

I don't know why I asked myself was I with you,
I wonder why I keep thinking of you,
There must be a reason why I'm still thinking of you,
It hurts me to this day to think of you.

I still haven't found out why I'm still thinking about you,
I'm thinking of you for all the good things when I was with you, Do I still think that I want to be with you?
You gave me some wonderful memories of what we did when I was with you.

Why did you have to break up with me?
Did you even like me,
If not then why where you even with me,
I wonder if you're life better now without me.

Do I Want To

If I saw you again, what would you say to me,
I don't care what you would say to me,
I am happy all alone on my own,
I think my life is better on my own.

Who said that I'm not missing you,
I really don't give a fuck about you,
What you have done to me, will forever more fucking hurt me,
Can I trust someone to fucking love me?

If I saw you again, what would I say to you,
I know what I would say to you,
I rather keep my thoughts and not say them to you,
I don't want to be with you.

Do I want to see you again for what you have done to me?
Do I want to see you again for being with me?
Why would I want to see you again for what you did to me?
It was a pleasure having you beside me.

I Wonder Who

I wonder who you like more him or me,
You wouldn't say that you did like me,
I wonder why you were with me,
I wonder who you like more him or me.

I wonder are you drinking more with him or was it more with me,
I couldn't tell if you were enjoying your drinking time with me,
I couldn't tell if you did fucking like me,
What were you even doing with me?

You said that you were happy that I could call you mine,
The two of us had agreed that was fine,
I felt that you didn't even love me,
I constantly asked you did you even love me.

You Were

You were there for me at the end of every call,
You and I were standing here in the hall,
You would pick me up from every fall,
I told you that one of my favourite authors was Roald Dahl.

I enjoyed our little phone calls during our time,
I didn't enjoy our little fights that we had throughout our time, Every time that we had a fight it would break my heart,
I knew that you didn't mean to break my heart.

You and I got to see Ed Sheeran sing,
You did tell me that you wanted a ring,
You and I went to Nando's to have some chicken wings,
The two of us did enjoy them chicken wings.

Christmas Day

When I was younger, I've always enjoyed Christmas Day,
I've always wanted that day to be every day,
I've always enjoyed opening all my Christmas presents on that day,
When I was younger, I was extremely delighted for Christmas day.

When I was younger, I've always enjoyed Christmas day,
I've always enjoyed my nice Christmas dinner on Christmas day, When I was younger, I've always wanted to go and see Man United play,
I will always remember when I got to see them play.

When I was younger, I've always wanted to know what everyone got me,
But I didn't want to peek at the Christmas presents that everyone got me,
I know that it would be wrong to peek at all the presents that everyone got me,
I've always remembered people saying, "oh what did you get me".

When I was younger, I've always went to my grandfathers for St. Stephen's Day,
I've always enjoyed going down to him on that day,
When I was younger, I've always wanted a football for Christmas day,
I've always wanted it just in case of a rainy day.

Christmas Day Acrostic

Christmas Day

Has

Reached us here just

In time as we

See

Thousands of people buying some last

Minute presents for

All their

Secret Santa presents and getting some

Decorations to hang up

Anywhere

You can put them

New Year's Day Acrostic

New Year's Day
Everywhere, all around the world
We see everyone counting down

Yet another brand-new year
Especially in years gone past of
All the hard times that we had in 2020 and 2021
Respectively we all done want to
See COVID-19 anymore or even hear of it again

Due to different reasons where we
All have
Yet we all don't want to remember the years we had COVID-19 for

I Saw You Standing

I saw you standing there with him,
I saw that you had a big smile one your face as you were with him,
I don't know why you didn't have the same smile on your face when you were with me,
I can see that you are in awe with him rather than me.

I saw that the two of us were having a good time,
I would like to know where you having a good time with me,
I know something was wrong when you did leave me,
I can say that the two of us did have a good time.

I would like to know are you even paying for halves of what he gets you,
I would like to know why you are with him,
I would like to know do you say to him I love you,
I would like to know what made you choose to be with him.

I would like to know why you left me,
What was it that made you leave me?
You didn't say to me that I love you,
I wonder why you didn't say I love you.

I Haven't Heard

I haven't heard you say that you loved me,
I thought that the two of us were going to say I love you all the time, I have been left waiting for you to say that you di love me, our relationship didn't work when you didn't say I love you all the time.

I haven't heard the reason why you left me,
Do I want to know the reason why you left me?
Why did I even love you?
I didn't even love you.

Mr. Meredith

You were a great teacher,

I got to see you in the school every day,

Every other teacher was saying that you were such a talented teacher,

I would quite regularly ask you how you were feeling every day.

I wonder do you like it now,

I do miss not seeing you,

Every time I listen to your music it reminds me of you,

I would do anything to have you back here now.

I Once Had You

I once had you,
I surprised myself when I was with you,
Did I like being with you,
Everyone knew that I was with you,

What was it that made me be with you?
Who said that I've never be with you?
 I don't know why I was spending my time being with you,
I knew that I didn't like you.

Cards Can Be

A card can be used for several events within a year,

A card can be used for birthdays where we all can have a beer,

A card can be used for funerals, where we all can share a tear,

A card can be used for weddings, where there could be so many of them in a year.

People are now using card instead of cash,

I know places that are still taking cash,

I thought that it would be easier to use card instead of cash,

What do you use card or cash?

Summer Acrostic

Summer in Ireland is

Unvindicable for

Many reasons which we all

Might agree on

Especially when we see

Rain falling for the summer in Ireland

Winter Acrostic

Winter has arrived

In Ireland as the

Nights are getting darker

Throughout each darker day we are seeing

Eventually horrible weather with a chance of

Rain or maybe snow

I Was With you

If I am there,
I was with you,
If I am there,
I was with you.

You were with me,
We lasted that long,
You were with me,
Did we last long.

I once had you,
You once had me,
Was I with you,
Where you with me.

Did I love you,
Did you love me,
You didn't love me,
I didn't love you.

Did you like me?

Did you like me,
Did I like you,
You didn't like me,
I didn't like you.

Our time lasted long,
How we lasted long,
Did you hate me,
You did hate me.

I saw you there,
You weren't with me,
I saw you there,
You weren't beside me.

You Really Surprised Me?

You really surprised me,
You were using me,
You were beside me,
You were using me.

You fucked it up,
Did you mean it,
You fucked it up,
Did you mean it.

Sometimes

Sometimes I do wonder I miss you,

I thought to myself that I couldn't believe that I was with you,

Sometimes I ask myself where did I go wrong,

Sometimes I think to myself was I in the wrong.

I couldn't see us lasting extremely long,

I don't know why we lasted so long,

Sometimes I glanced across of some old photos of the two of us being together, it put a smile on my face,

When I was I with you I always had a smile on my face.

Sometimes I thought that I wasn't supposed to be with you,

Sometimes I wonder why did I really love you,

I do wonder why I miss you,

I do wonder did I really fucking love you.

I Saw You There?

I saw you there,
You saw me there,
Did you see me,
Did you hate me.

Did you see me,
Did I see you,
Did I love you,
Did you hate me.

You didn't love you,
Did you love me,
You did love me,
Did you love me.

I Have What You Don't Have?

I have what you don't have,

I guess that I could say that I was shy,

You have what I don't have,

I guess that you were right about me being shy.

I have what you don't need,

You have what I don't need,

I guess that I could've left you,

If I did that I wouldn't of still being with you.

I was there for you all the time,

You were also there for me all the time,

Didn't you like me,

Or didn't you not like me.

What was I doing with you,

If you didn't enjoy your time being with me,

Did I enjoy my time whilst I was with you,

What was it that you didn't see in me.

There Was

There was a time that I didn't love you,
There was a time that I didn't love you,
There was a time that I forgot to say 'I love you",
There was a time that you didn't say "I love you".

There was a time that I didn't care about being with you,
There was a time that you didn't love me,
There was a reason why I didn't love you,
There was so many reasons why you didn't love me.

I could tell that you couldn't last that long with me,
I noticed that you hated being with me in the first place,
I didn't know why you were with me I the first place,
Why where you with me if you hated being with me.

I Sit Here

I sit here all alone on my own,

I sit here wondering what made me be here on my own,

I thought to myself is it better on my own,

I thought to myself it could be better all alone on my own.

I drink by myself to cope with all the things that I've done,

The more I drink it helps me forget all the things that I've done,

I think to myself what have I done,

I would want to turn the clock back to prevent us from doing the things that I've done.

I thought that there was a time that we had each other,

There was a time that we did hate each other,

What made us hate each other,

I don't know why we did hate each other.

Was I Supposed To?

Was I supposed to be with you,
I wasn't supposed to be with you,
I can't even remember what made me ask you to be with me,
I can't even remember if you loved me.

I can't even remember if you did like me,
I do remember that you did fucking use me,
I was heartbroken hearing that you did leave me,
I was unsure if you did even enjoy your time whilst being with me.

I Thought Being With You?

I thought being with you meant everything to me,

I thought being with you made you feel that you actually loved me,

I wasn't expecting you not to love me,

I did you say that you did you love me.

Maybe I was with you to please you,

Maybe I was with you to see would you say " I love you',

There wasn't any issues with you until left me,

Who cared about if you even loved me?.

I've Seen You

I seen you there tonight beside me,
I saw you there tonight beside me,
I seen you there every other day beside me,
I saw you the every other night beside me,
You saw us there together beside each other,
You seen us there together beside each other,
You used to enjoy your time once you were with me,
I would often ask you did you enjoy your time with me,
I would often ask you did you love me,
I would often ask you what made you even love me,
I could assume that you didn't love me,
Was I right that you didn't even love me.

Printed in Poland
by Amazon Fulfillment
Poland Sp. z o.o., Wrocław